SAINT PAUL
PUBLIC LIBRARY

green
books

Thanks to the library, these gently
used books are available
for **free** for your family.

Everyone who spends time with children, especially young children from 0-5 years old,
should talk, read, and write with them. Children see that reading is important when
they see you read. Talk about pictures in books, show children how to turn the pages,
and encourage them to ask questions.

TALK. READ. WRITE.

Edited by Hazel Chan
Design by Nancy Field

Photo credit: Page 34, Polaris by Paul Mandel

Library of Congress Cataloging-in-Publication Data

Dispezio, Michael A.
Map mania : discovering where you are and getting to where you
aren't / by Michael A. DiSpezio.
  p. cm.
Includes index.
ISBN 0-8069-4407-2
1. Map drawing–Juvenile literature. 2. Map reading–Juvenile literature.
[1. Map drawing. 2. Map reading. 3. Maps.] I. Title.

GA130.D65   2001
912–dc21   2001020773

10   9   8   7   6   5   4   3   2   1

Published by Sterling Publishing Company, Inc.
387 Park Avenue South, New York, N.Y. 10016

© 2002 by Michael A. DiSpezio

Distributed in Canada by Sterling Publishing
c/o Canadian Manda Group, One Atlantic Avenue, Suite 105
Toronto, Ontario, Canada M6K 3E7

Distributed in Great Britain and Europe by Chris Lloyd at Orca Book
Services, Stanley House, Fleets Lane, Poole BH15 3AJ, England.

Distributed in Australia by Capricorn Link (Australia) Pty Ltd.
P.O. Box 704, Windsor, NSW 2756, Australia

Sterling ISBN 0-8069-4407-2

Table of Contents

Have You Ever Been Lost?

Real lost. So lost that you had no idea where you were or where you were going. Perhaps you looked around, trying to get your bearings. Right. Left. Back. Front. Up. Down. But nothing was familiar.

You had to make a decision. Should you keep going ahead or turn around and retrace your steps?

There was no one to ask. You had to decide…alone. And to make matters worse, it was getting dark. *Real dark.*

Well, don't worry because right now, you're not lost. You're here. Well, actually, you're not *here*. You're really *there*, *out there* reading this book. If you were *here*, you'd be a particle of ink or a piece of paper on this page. Right?

Sounds confusing? But it's a lot less mind-boggling than getting lost. And that's what this book is all about: getting lost and how to keep from doing it.

Halls of Horror

Think back to your first day at a new school. It can be a pretty scary experience. New teachers, new friends, and the scariest thing of all—a new place.

You don't want to get lost on your first day because:

#1. *It's a mega waste of time.*

While your classmates are completing the warm-up problem, you're walking in circles. By the time you find the classroom, everyone has learned how to add negative numbers-everyone that is, except you. Now, you're really lost!

#2. *No need to risk looking dorky.*

It's difficult to look cool when everyone knows that it was only you who couldn't figure out that, like most street numbers, the even numbers (2, 4, 6, etc.) were on one side of the hall, odd numbers (1, 3, 5, etc.) on the other.

#3. *Brainless bullies terrorize the empty halls.*

Better stay away! Better know your way around! Better not get lost!

WHAT'S THE BEST WAY TO KEEP FROM GETTING LOST IN A NEW SCHOOL?

a) Hire a psychic advisor.
b) Use a compass.
c) Read a map.

If you picked "a," you've been watching too much television or reading too many supermarket tabloids. Sorry, but psychic advisors can't help here.

If you picked "b," be prepared (as the Scouts say). Although a compass may help locate the lost City of Petra, it really isn't the best way to find the cafeteria.

If you picked "c," congratulations! A map is a guide. It shows where you are, and where you're not. So before you wander unfamiliar hallways, it might not be a bad idea to study a map that shows the layout of your school. If there is no such map, why not volunteer to create one for new students? Your teachers and school administrators could really appreciate your efforts. The type of map you'll be making is called a floor plan.

Making Your Own Floor Plan

THINGS YOU'LL NEED:

- Sheet of graph paper
- Pencil
- Ruler
- Floor
- A desire to crawl through cobwebs, find old misplaced moldy Halloween candy from last year, and take measurements at really weird angles.

WHAT YOU'LL HAVE TO DO:

Pick a room. Although any room will do, it's probably best to start small.

Measure the length of each wall in your chosen room. Some walls are easy to measure. Others require a bit of creative wall walking. Write down all your measurements. Once you have them, get out your blank sheet of graph paper. The next step is to

shrink your room measurements onto the grids of the graph paper. Here's how. If you live in the U.S. (and don't care to impress your metric-minded science teacher), you probably wrote down your measurements in feet. O.K. We figured that you'd do that and so we designed the grid with that in mind.

To keep things simple, make each box of the grid represent one square foot of space. Remember, we're talking square foot as in area (not as in some alien body part). So if your bedroom wall is 5 feet long, you'll draw this wall as a straight line that stretches across five boxes. Likewise, a 3-foot wall stretches across three boxes. Note that unless you live in a giant teapot, fuel storage tank, or flying saucer, you'll find the graph's lines ideal for helping show straight walls and room corners.

The final room outline should just about fill the graph paper. If you have extra space, you can draw in the room next door. Once the outline of the room is complete, decide on other things to add to your floor plan. Remember, this map is your on-paper representation of reality. You get to pick what's in your drawing, such as windows, chairs, or lamps.

FILLING IT IN

Now that you know how this thing works, why not create a floor plan for more than just one room, such as an entire apartment, a multiroom camper, or one floor of a house? First, measure the outer walls of the whole place. (Remember, when you put this outline on paper, use a large enough sheet of paper to accommodate the whole layout.) Next, draw in the other walls; then fill in the inside room-by-room.

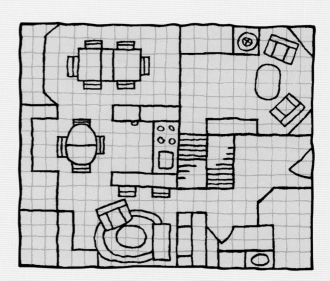

Making Your Own Map

Look out the front door of your house or building. What do you see?

Most likely, there's some sort of street or road. So take a field trip. Seriously. Leave your house (with a parent, if necessary) and walk out onto the street. Keep walking and you'll discover at least one other street. As you continue walking, you'll run into more streets and more streets and more streets. Get the picture?

BIRD'S-EYE VIEW

Now imagine this picture from high above. Think of how it might appear to a bird, such as a hawk or an eagle.

Pretend you're the bird soaring overhead. Look down and check out the scenery. Assuming you're not hung up on searching for mice, moles, or other hairy hors d'oeuvre, you'll appreciate a really neat layout of streets, houses, sidewalks, and trees.

It's this bird's-eye view that's shown on street maps.

MAP QUIZ

The box that contains the explanations for map symbols is called:

a) a key.
b) a legend.

Did you pick "a"? If so, great job. You are correct!

Did you pick "b"? If so, great job. You are correct!

Most of the time, mapmakers can make a clear cut decision. "That way is north." "This way is south." "I need to find my car." However, when it comes to naming the box of symbols, they can't make up their mind. So, to be fair-minded, the box can be called a key or a legend. Two names in one!

SCALE SCALE SCALE

Most keys (or legends) have something that indicates how much the mapmaker has shrunk down reality to fit it onto the map. This gauge is called a scale. Some scales are described with words like "1 inch equals 1 mile." Other scales use bars that look like this:

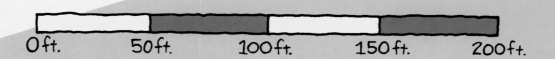

0 ft.   50 ft.   100 ft.   150 ft.   200 ft.

Ready? Draw.

Now that you know what it takes, it's time to map out your street or neighborhood block. First, you'll need to draw a bird's-eye view of your house. Since you probably can't fly over your home, you'll need to "invent" this view. Here's how:

Marking Your House
Go outside (and don't forget to bring this book with you). Stand back and get a wide view of your house. Look down the street. Look up the street. Try to imagine what is on the other side of your house. Can you figure out what's around the corner?

You'll build your map on graph paper. Select a square in the center of the grid of the graph paper. That square will represent your house.

If you live in a mostly square building (the dimensions, not the occupants), you should darken one graph box to represent your home.

If you live in a building that looks more rectangular, use two boxes.

If you live in an "L-shaped" building, use three boxes make this shape.

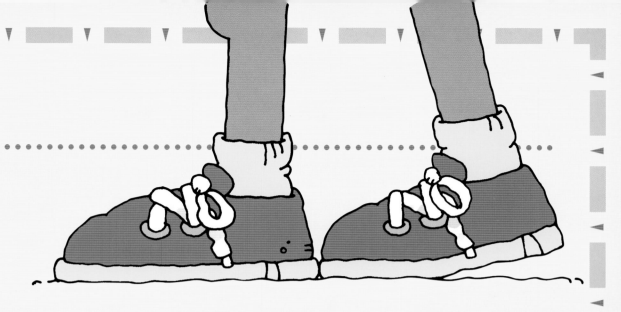

Taking Measurements

To do this, we'll use the ever popular step-by-step method. Just count the number of steps that it takes to walk from corner to corner along the front of your house. Record this distance. It will be your "scale" to the map. If your house was twenty steps long, then the side of one grid box equals twenty steps.

Walk from the front your house to the end of your street. Say it took sixty steps. That means that the map distance from your house to that end of the street is three boxes. Suppose it took a hundred steps to walk from your house to the other end of the street. On the map, this distance would stretch across five boxes.

Once your street is drawn, add the remaining houses on your street. When the houses are finished, take a step back. Do you live on a block? If so, does it have a square or rectangular shape? Start walking. Count the number of steps that it takes to walk along the block's three other sides. With these measurements, complete the block map.

Finishing Your Map

Keep expanding your map. Eventually, you'll get bored or run out of grid space. That's when the map outline is complete.

Now it's time to decorate your map. You don't have to be an artist. You can color in lawns, sidewalks, playgrounds, cars, and fields. Use symbols to represent trees, street lamps, garbage cans, and fire hydrants (with or without dogs).

Street Smarts

KNOW YOUR STREET

1. When streets were first named, most were dubbed after a:
a) number
b) landmark
c) type of tree
d) letter

2. Homer and Marge Simpson live on which Springfield street?
a) Main Street
b) Pine Street
c) Easy Street
d) Evergreen Terrace

3. Who doesn't belong?
a) Snuffleupagus
b) Lambchop
c) Kermit
d) Elmo

4. Sherlock Holmes lived on:
a) Fleet Street
b) Butcher Street
c) Baker Street
d) Downing Street

5. Which character might you find on Privet Drive?
a) Nancy Drew
b) Charlie Brown
c) Forest Gump
d) Harry Potter

Answer on page 79.

ROYAL PAVEMENT

In the 1200s, King Augustus tried something new. He had the street that ran in front of his Paris castle paved with stones. Although this new surface made travel easier, it wasn't the King's main motive for surfacing the street.

Can you guess why he did it?

a) His wife's sister was an unemployed stone cutter who needed the work.
b) The King was an avid skate border in need of a nearby track.
c) It was a way to stop the street from being used as a sewer and outhouse.

Answer on page 79.

TWO OF A KIND

Check out these cities, streets, and walking places.
Can you pair each place with the city in which it's found?

Champs-Elysées	London
Broadway	Beijing
Pennsylvania Avenue	Washington
St. Mark's Square	Los Angeles
Piccadilly Circus	Paris
Sunset Boulevard	New York City
Tiananmen Square	Venice

Answer on page 79

A New Direction

BIRTH OF THE COMPASS (OR, AN HISTORIC ORIENTATION)

Around 2000 years ago, Chinese seafarers first used the magnetic needle in navigation. At about the same time, many Europeans had a slightly different view of magnets. They believed that the natural magnet (called lodestone) had dark forces and magical powers. Even as late as the 1600s, Europeans had weird thoughts about magnets. How weird?

- Love potions that contain bits of magnetic rock are guaranteed to bring separated lovers back together.
- Touching a magnet or lodestone with a diamond wipes out its magnetic power.
- A huge mountain of lodestone exists way up north. Its magnetic field is so strong enough that it can rip the iron nails right out of a ship's hull!
- Some people own special types of magnets that attract fish.
- Onion and garlic breath is a sure way to destroy a magnet's power.

A TALE OF TWO POLES

Spin a basketball on your finger. The spot where your finger supports the spin is the ball's geographic South Pole. Likewise, the opposite spot on the top of the ball is its geographic North Pole.

   The spinning Earth has the same type of poles. Imagine that you could go to the arctic and stand on the north geographic pole. About 1000 miles from this pole is another pole. This other pole has nothing to do with spinning. It's the North magnetic Pole. The North magnetic Pole "sits" as if it were positioned atop of a magnet that stretched for thousands of miles through the inside of the Earth. When you take a compass reading, the needle points to the Earth's magnetic pole, not the geographic one.

North Geographic Pole

North Magnetic Pole

South Geographic Pole

South Magnetic Pole

ALL Stars
3

Time for Navigation Tools

Host: What time is it?

Audience: It's Time for Navigation Tools!

Host: That's right. It's the TV show that explores the tools of navigators.

Cohost: Today, we're going to dig back in time and build a model of an early compass.

Host: To build this baby, you'll need a steel sewing needle, clear container, water, bar magnet, and plastic foam cup.

Cohost: You don't need the whole cup-just a piece of the flat bottom will do. You can use scissors to poke through the cup and separate this bottom from the top.

Host: To magnetize the needle, stroke the magnet across the needle's length about twenty times.

Cohost: But do not stroke the needle back and forth. The magnet should always move along the needle in only one direction.

Host: Now lay the needle on the foam "raft." It should look like this:

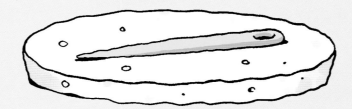

Cohost: Fill a clear container about one-third full of water. Then place it over the compass rose that's below. That's right, place it directly on this book. A compass rose is a layout that shows different directions.

Host: Lower the needle "raft" into the center of the container. It should spin freely and stop moving when the needle points North.

Cohost: To be really cool, swing the book around so the North of the compass rose points in the same direction as the magnetized needle.

Compass Basics

Have you ever bought cereal just to get the prize buried at the bottom of the package? Do you have a collection of unopened party favors? Do you trade in arcade points for bottom-shelf prizes? If so, congratulations. You are probably the proud owner of a compass!

There are two types of compasses*, the fixed dial compass and the orienteering compass. (We'll discuss the orienteering compass on page 22.)

FIXED DIAL COMPASS

A fixed dial compass is the simplest (and usually the cheapest) compass. It is the no-frills model. It consists of a magnetized needle that balances and rotates on a pin-like support. The spinning needle is housed in a container that has a clear (and non-movable) plastic top. Through this cover, you can observe the action of the needle as it spins over regions labeled North, South, East, and West.

*Three, if you count the drawing tool that creates arcs and circles

---

Challenge Break

What is a cardinal direction?
a) The path followed by a migrating red bird.
b) Slide, steal, bunt, and other signals given by St. Louis baseball coaches.
c) North, South, East, and West.

The answer is "c." Cardinal directions are the four basic directions: North, South, East, and West. On the compass, these directions are called *points* and are represented by the letters N, S, E, and W.

MORE TO THE POINT

Take at look at your compass. The points N, S, E, and W are printed in the compass. Between these cardinal directions, you can have other letters, such as SE (Southeast) or NW (Northwest). These letters represent directions that are in between the cardinal points.

Sometimes a compass may have numbers that range from 0 to 360. The numbers represent measurements called *degrees*. Unlike the degrees in a thermometer, which

(and Basic Compasses)

tell you what's the temperature outside, the compass degrees indicate direction.

The ring of your compass has 360 of these degrees. Most of the time 360 is not shown, because it's the same direction as 0 degrees. To keep things simple, the highest printed number is 330, but you can count the degree marks all the way up to 360 if you want.

Here's how some of the major degree measurements stack up:

0 degrees = North
90 degrees = East
180 degrees = South
270 degrees = West
36,000,000 degrees = the Sun
(hot joke—only kidding).

USING A COMPASS

1. Stand away from any metal objects, motors, magnets, and electrical wires.
2. Hold the compass flat so that the needle rotates freely.
3. Once the needle stops, its red tip (or gray, if you're color-blind) points to magnetic North.
4. Gently rotate the housing beneath the needle so that the North on the compass rose aligns with the direction indicated by the red tip of the needle.
5. Once it's aligned, you can use the numbers to identify the degree measurements to various landmarks.

The Orienteering Compass

Like the fixed dial compass, the basic part of this orienteering compass is a magnetized needle. It too has a North-pointing red end. But there's more. It has a whole bunch of adult-impressing numbers and a movable dial. These numbers and dial make this compass easier to use when reading maps, charting trails, and staying on course.

GETTING THE JITTERS OUT

Unlike the fixed dial compass, the orienteering compass doesn't waste any time. Within moments, it quickly settles, stops, and points (without jittering) to North.

The compass doesn't have the jitters because the inside of the capsule is filled with a stabilizing liquid. It provides a thicker surrounding than plain air that's in the fixed dial compass. This "thickness" cushions the needle's movement to reduce its jitters.

"RUFF" LIKENESS

Your orienteering compass has two moving parts: The needle and the capsule. The needle moves by itself with a little help from the Earth's magnetic field. The capsule moves when you turn it. This way, you can "lock" in and remember a direction.

Take a close look at the capsule. Do you see the outline of the arrow that's printed on the capsule? That outline is often called the "doghouse." Does it look like a doghouse? No way: It looks like the outline of a needle. However, the capsule "doghouse" looks more like a doghouse than the magnetic needle looks like a dog. "Ruff" likeness.

CHALLENGE YOUR MEMORY

Come in Tower...

1. Place a model or paper airplane in the corner of your room. Imagine that the airplane marks Runway 19 of Sterling City Airport.

2. Stand in the far opposite corner of the room. You are the navigator of a jet coming in for a landing. The pilot's voice crackles over the headphones, "Find out the course heading that will bring us to Runway One-Niner at SCA."

3. To determine this heading, hold the compass in your right hand, just above your waist. Aim the bearing arrow at the runway. The bearing arrow doesn't move, so you use it to aim at your target.

4. Look at the magnetic needle. Most likely, it isn't pointing in the same direction as the fixed bearing arrow. It might be pointing to the right, left, back, or wherever.

5. Here's where the memory part comes in. It's called placing the needle in the doghouse. While keeping the bearing arrow aimed at the runway, spin the capsule so that the needle is placed within its outline. (Remember, the outline was called the doghouse.)

6. Once this direction has been locked in, your compass "remembers" the heading to the runway.

7. Look at the intersection where the bearing arrow meets the degree measurements. This degree reading is your heading. It is the direction that you must travel in order to reach the airport.

8. To test it, don't look up. Keep the compass cradled at your waist, straight ahead of you. Move slowly in the direction of the bearing arrow. Adjust your path so that the needle always remains in the doghouse. If you don't trip over any toys or piles of clothing, you should get pretty close to the runway.

Showing Off

Now that you know what you're doing, let's show off your skills outside!

Step 1. Field Trip Time
Get a pen and paper, and go to the local ball field. Stroll out onto the pitcher's mound. To lessen the chance of getting clunked on the head with a baseball, make sure that no teams are using the ball field at the time.

Step 2. Heading Home
Stand on the pitcher's mound. Hold the compass in your right hand just above your waist. Aim the bearing arrow at home plate. Keep the compass level and pointed directly at the plate. Rotate the capsule to *place the needle in the doghouse*. Make sure that the bearing arrow still points directly at home plate.

Look at the rose of the compass. The intersection between the bearing arrow and the rose identifies *the* degree heading to home plate. Mark this heading on your sheet of paper.

Step 3. Getting to Second Base
While you're still at the mound, turn around and aim the bearing arrow at second base. Repeat what you did in Step 2 to obtain a heading to second base. Record this heading on the same paper.

Step 4. First and Third
There are only two bases left: first and third. Use your orienteering compass (and what you learned in step 2) to get the heading from the pitcher's mound to these two bases. Don't forget to record these headings.

By now, you should see some sort of number thing with the headings to the bases. Each heading should differ from its closest neighbor by 90 degrees—just like the cardinal points on a compass.

TRY TRIANGULATING

One of the compass's best tricks is its ability to triangulate (try-ANG-you-late), which means finding an exact location without using a map! Let's go back to our local ball field (not during a game) to practice this skill.

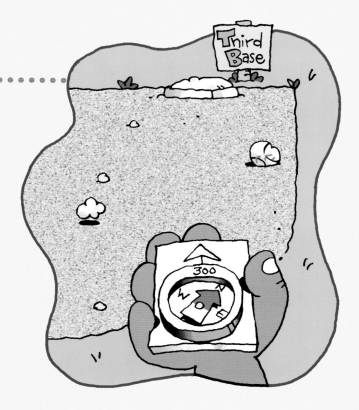

1. Get lost in right, center, or left field. Find a nice place in the dirt and name your "spot."
2. Hold the compass in your right hand just above your waist. Aim the bearing arrow at third base. Keep the compass level and pointed directly at the base.
3. Now, it's time to *place the needle in the doghouse*. Slowly turn the capsule so that the needle outline "frames" the magnetic needle. Make sure that the bearing arrow still points at third base.
4. Look at the rose of the compass. The intersection where the bearing arrow crosses the rose is the *bearing* to third base. Write down this degree heading.
5. Don't move. Get the degree heading to first base by repeating Steps 2 through 4. Write down this bearing.

6. It's done. These two bearings are all that you'll need to return to your "spot." There is no other spot on this ball field (or anywhere on the planet) that has the same two bearings to first and third base.

Come On Back and Visit Sometime

Whenever you wish to return to your spot, just stroll the outfield. Keep taking bearings to first and third base. When the bearings to the bases match what you've written down, you've returned to your special place.

The Parking Lot:
A Lost World

Have you ever been with someone who "lost" a car in the never-ending parking lot of a shopping mall?

You know the story. You arrive at the mall and park in the middle of an empty parking lot. After a few hours of shopping (plus a movie, plus a pizza) you walk out of the mall. You look into the parking lot and you are HORRIFIED! The lot is packed full of thousands of cars—most of them the same make and color as the one you parked. You'll never get home!

You remind the driver that if they would have let you bring your orienteering compass, none of this would have happened. Here's why:

1. Upon arriving at an empty parking lot, select two tall landmarks. Lampposts or buildings work great.
2. Get the exact location of your position by taking a "fix" to each landmark. When explaining your actions to adults, don't hesitate to use the word "triangulate." They're easily impressed.
3. Once you've made two fixes, write down the names of the landmarks and the heading to each. Store this paper in your pocket.
4. Enjoy your day at the mall. Have pizza. See a movie.
5. When you exit the mall, remove the heading paper. While keeping an eye out for moving vehicles (and wandering shopping carts), take the bearings of two landmarks. When the bearings match what you've written down, you've returned to your parking space. Yes, this is your parking spot. But where is your car?

The Nose Knows

Which of the following things are in your nose?

a) A wobbling rod that can locate water
b) A milk bubble from sixth grade
c) A compass

The answer is "c." Although it doesn't look it, your nose contains a compass. Well, kind of.

You see, the bone in the middle of your nose contains a trace of iron. Although the amount of iron is small, it can "sense" the Earth's magnetic field. Tests have shown that some people can use this built-in compass to locate the direction of our planet's magnetic North Pole.

WE ARE NOT ALONE!

Some bacteria that live in soil also have a compass in their nose (well, more accurately, *somewhere* in their bodies, since they really don't have any noses). These bacteria contain tiny grains of iron. Scientists think that these simple forms of life use the iron to uncover the direction of the North Pole.

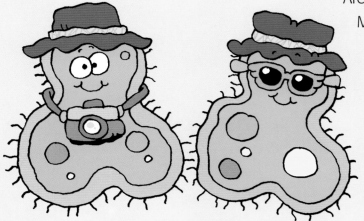

You may ask, "Why? Are the bacteria going on vacation to the Canadian lakes? Are they looking to photograph the Cariboo Mountains?" Probably not.

It's thought that by knowing the direction of North, bacteria can figure out something really important (to them anyway): Which way is the surface. By knowing which way is "up," these bacteria can keep their wandering to the best hotel and restaurant places for microbes.

WEIRD, BUT TRUE SCIENCE DEPARTMENT

Did you know that the North magnetic Pole doesn't stay put? From year to year, it moves across the surface of the Earth. Right now it's up in the arctic, about 1000 miles from the geographic North Pole. But about 1000 years ago, it was in central Asia. Three hundred years later, it danced around the Pacific. These days, however, its wandering is confined to the icy regions of the far North.

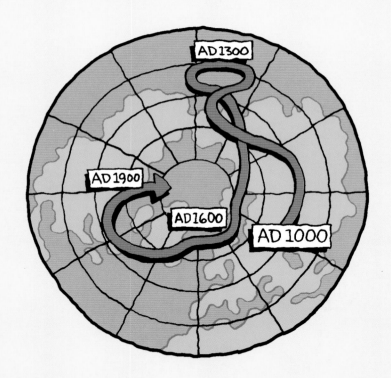

The different positions of the North magnetic Pole. Imagine you're above the Earth and looking down on the North Pole.

Only the Shadow Knows

SIDEWALK SHADOW STICK

Follow the steps below to construct a really cool tool. It's a type of direction pointer called a shadow stick. Here's how to build it:

1. Find a straight stick that's about as long as your forearm.
2. Jam the stick into soft ground (don't break it!) or support it so that it stands upright by itself.
3. Mark the spot where the stick's shadow ends.
4. Wait about 20 minutes.
5. Take a look at where the stick's shadow now ends. Mark this second spot.
6. Draw a line from the first mark to this second mark. This line indicates the West-to-East direction. The first mark is West. The second mark is East.
7. Now draw a perpendicular line right through the middle of this line. The new line indicates the North/South direction.

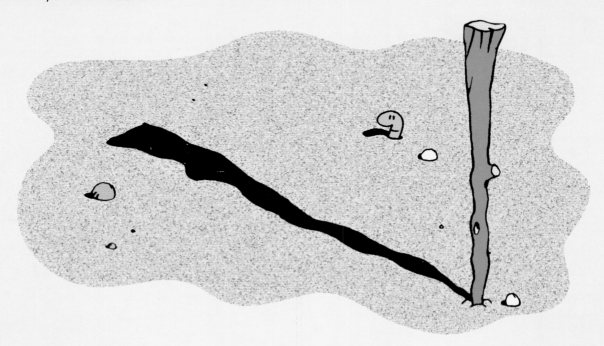

Almost Always ... Maybe ... Sorta ... It Depends

Although the Sun does appear to rise in the East and set in the West, these directions are only close calls. Most of the time, the Sun's position and path only approximate East/West directions. Therefore, the shadow stick produces a pretty good (but not exact) representation of the cardinal directions.

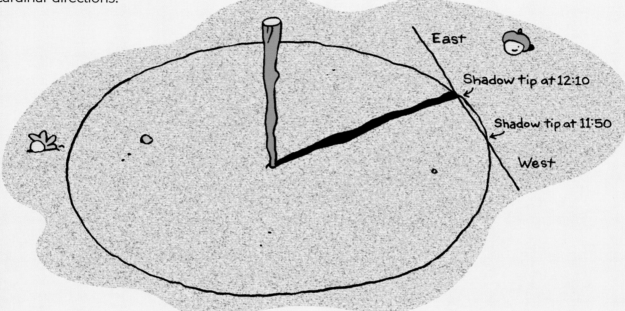

East

Shadow tip at 12:10

Shadow tip at 11:50

West

EVEN BETTER

Do you want to increase the accuracy of the shadow stick? Ten minutes before high noon, mark the tip of the stick's shadow length. Draw a circle around the stick. The circle uses the base of the stick as its center. The radius of the circle is the distance from the stick base to the shadow tip. As noontime approaches, the shadow will shrink. After passing noon, the shadow will get longer and eventually touch the other side of the circle. Place a second mark at this spot. Now, connect the two marks. This line forms a more accurate east-west line. And again, if you draw a perpendicular line right through the middle of this line, the new line indicates the North/South direction. Neat, eh?

Natural (but Imperfect) Compasses

Look up. If it's daytime and you live North of the equator, the Sun isn't directly overhead. Instead, it hangs in the Southern sky. The amount of "hang" depends upon both the season and the time.

Now imagine the sun as a really big flashlight. Its rays will strike the South side of Northern Hemisphere objects such as buildings, trees, and people. Although the heated air spreads out the Sun's warmth, surfaces that directly face the Sun get more sunshine than those that face away.

Moss, like other green plants, enjoys humid regions. Since the Sun dries out the South side of the tree trunks, moss grows on the parts of a tree that are more apt to remain in shade. That's why moss tends to be found on the North side of tree trunks, but that's *not* always the case.

OOPS! ACCEPTING THE EXCEPTION

Moss can also prefer the South side of tree trunks! That's because there are other factors that influence its growth. Things like prevailing wind, nutrients, light, and other plants can create an environment in which moss grows equally on all sides of the trunk.

Before using moss as a compass, check out the local tree trunks. Do they have more growth on one side? Although moss growth may not point to North, as you travel, any change in the moss's growing side may mean that you "changed" direction! So as an early warning system, moss is a great thing to check out and keep your eye on.

ECHO LOCATOR

Did you know that echoes can sometimes be used to uncover directions?

Drop something heavy over a mountainside. (If you don't have a mountainside handy, just imagine.) The sound of its crash travels outwards in all directions. If the sound waves strike a dry, hard surface, a strong echo returns. In contrast, sounds that strike a soft, mushy surface are less likely to be reflected.

In the Northern Hemisphere, the Sun is more likely to dry out the bark of the South facing side of tree trunks. Therefore, the direction from which the strongest echo returns tends to be South. But remember, other factors can affect this echo direction. For example, the twists and turns in a valley can ricochet echoes and make them sound as if they came from different directions. Even the type of ground surface can play tricks and affect the sound's rebound.

Seeing Stars

Go outside and look up at the night sky. What do you see? Well, it depends on what hemisphere you're in.

If you live in the Northern Hemisphere, keep reading. If you live in the Southern Hemisphere, feel free to jump to "When the Dipper dips too low" on page 38. It's a Southern Hemispherian's view of the night-time sky.

STAR GAZING FOR NORTHERN HEMISPHERIANS

If the Sun has gone down and the night is clear, you'll probably see some stars. Among the thousands of stars that fill the sky, one is especially useful for finding your way in the Northern Hemisphere. That star is Polaris, a.k.a. (also known as) the North Star.

What Makes Polaris So Special?
It is the only star in the Northern sky that appears to remain in the same spot. Through the night, all other stars appear to move along a curved path. Only Polaris remains fixed.

Who Left the Shutter Open?

This picture was taken by a camera that was aimed upwards into the nighttime sky. Instead of a "quick click "the shutter remained open for hours. During this expo-sure, all the stars, except one, traced out their circular path. The only star that did not move appeared as a dot. This star is Polaris. It remained fixed at the center of the star spin.

Not only does Polaris stay still, but it "hangs" due North in the nighttime sky. Locate Polaris and you have an instant compass.

THE BIG DIPPER

Your key to locating the North Star is first finding the Big Dipper. Why the Big Dipper? Because it's BIG, has a funny name, and is an easy shape to recognize.

The Big Dipper is made up of seven distinct stars. If you hold your hand up to "measure" the night sky (see illustration), the Big Dipper stars extends across the sky about the distance from the tip of your thumb to the tip of your little finger.

Whether you see the Big Dipper right-side up or upside down depends on the season. Suppose you looked for the Big Dipper early in the evening. During the summer, the "cup" is at the bottom of this constellation. During the spring, the dipper is upside down. In the winter, the cup is at the top. Only during summer months does the Big Dipper appear right-side up.

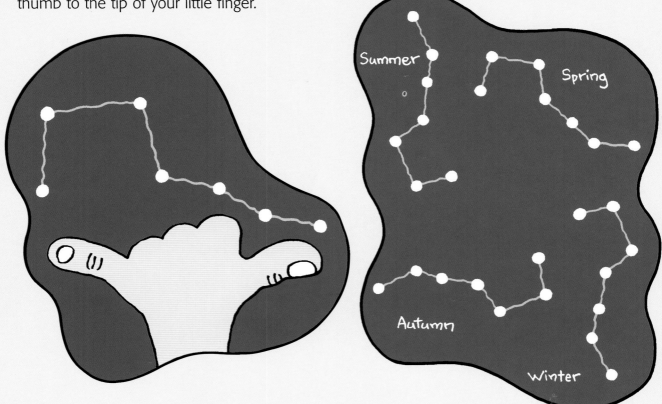

The North Star

FINDING POLARIS

The Big Dipper has two stars, Merak (ME-rack) and Dubhe (DU-bee). They are located in the cup of the dipper. An arrow drawn from Merak to Dubhe will point you to Polaris.

Polaris belongs to its own dipper-like constellation called the Little Dipper. It too is formed from seven stars. Unlike the Big Dipper, the Little Dipper is difficult to find. Even if you are looking right at it, you may not see it. That's why the "direction line" is a great way to uncover Polaris.

Polaris is the last star in the handle of the Little Dipper. Starting from Dubhe, if you hold your hand up to "measure" the night sky (see illustration), Polaris is located about the distance from the tip of your thumb to the tip of your little finger.

Summer

Summer is a comfortable time to stargaze, but it's the worst time to find the Big Dipper. During the summer months, this constellation is low in the sky. In many places, ground lights and objects along the horizon block the stars from view.

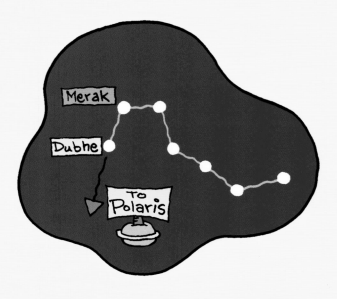

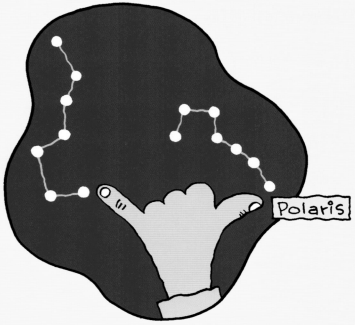

Backup Plan

There's another summer constellation that "points" the way to Polaris. It's called Cassiopeia, and this star group looks like an upper case "M." The middle of this constellation points downward to Polaris. Look for Cassiopeia's distinct shape higher in the sky than the Little Dipper.

When the Dipper Dips Too Low
(equal time for South Hemispherians)

Although Polaris is a great directional star for regions North of the equator, it's difficult to use if you live in (or travel to) the Southern Hemisphere. That's because something blocks your view. That something is called Planet Earth.

LOOKING THE OTHER WAY!

So what can you do if you live south of the equator? Look the other way.

In the Northern Hemisphere, Polaris remains fixed directly above our planet's North geographic Pole. In the Southern Hemisphere, no such sky marker exists!

For the most part, the Southern sky contains fewer bright stars and less noticeable constellations. To find the spot that is positioned straight out from the South geographic Pole, you'll need to locate it with the chart on the opposite page.

As you can see, the spot (called the South celestial point) is found in the middle between the constellation triangulum and a fuzzy collection of lights called the Large Magellanic Cloud.

Just like the Northern variety, the spot points out a cardinal direction. It hangs due South. So whether you're in Australia or Argentina, it's this point that can help you find you way.

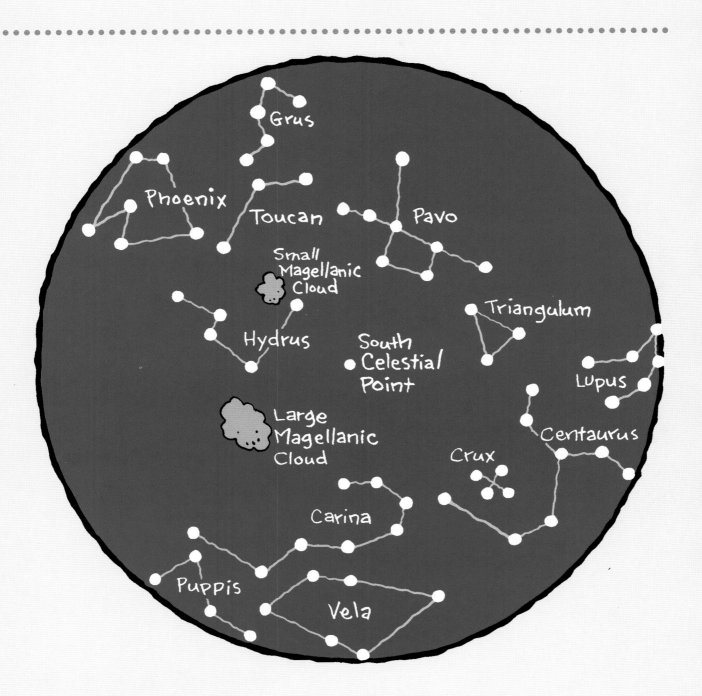

Getting Unlost: The Celestial Fix

You are lost in the middle of nowhere. It's nighttime. The stars are out. You don't have a compass, but you do have a map. As your flashlight dims, you study the map. Before the light dies out, you realize that you need to travel due East.

How do you find due East? First, we need to make a couple of assumptions. Assumption #1: You own this book and have read the previous pages that explain how to find the North or South celestial point. Assumption #2: You are lost in either the Northern or Southern Hemisphere (a pretty sure bet).

FOR ANY PLACE IN THE NORTHERN HEMISPHERE

Locate Polaris. You can use any of the star tricks you learned on pages 34–37. Unless you are standing directly atop of the North geographic pole, Polaris isn't straight up in the sky. It hangs down. The closer you are to the Equator, the lower it hangs. The closer to the North Pole, the higher up it is.

Turn your body so that you face Polaris. You are now facing not only this guiding star, but you are also facing due North. Hold both arms out to your sides. Your right arm points due East. Your left arm points West. Your spine points South.

Identify a landmark that your right arm points to. Begin walking. Every once in a while, check your direction by getting another "fix" from the North Star.

FOR ANY PLACE IN
THE SOUTHERN HEMISPHERE

Use the map of the Southern sky found on page 39 to locate the South celestial point. Unless you are standing directly atop of the South geographic pole, that point isn't straight up in the sky. It hangs down. The closer you are to the Equator, the lower it hangs.

Turn your body so that you face the South celestial point. You are now facing not only this guiding star, but you are also facing due South. Hold both arms out to your sides. Your right arm points due West. Your left arm points East. Your spine points North.

Identify a landmark that your left arm points to. Begin walking. Every once in a while, check your direction by getting another "fix" from the nighttime sky.

Historical Side Trip

Even before there were roads, wrong turns, and rest stops, there were maps. The first maps were nothing more than lines drawn in the dirt. These scratches might have showed the location of a cave, village, or popular hangout for woolly mammoths.

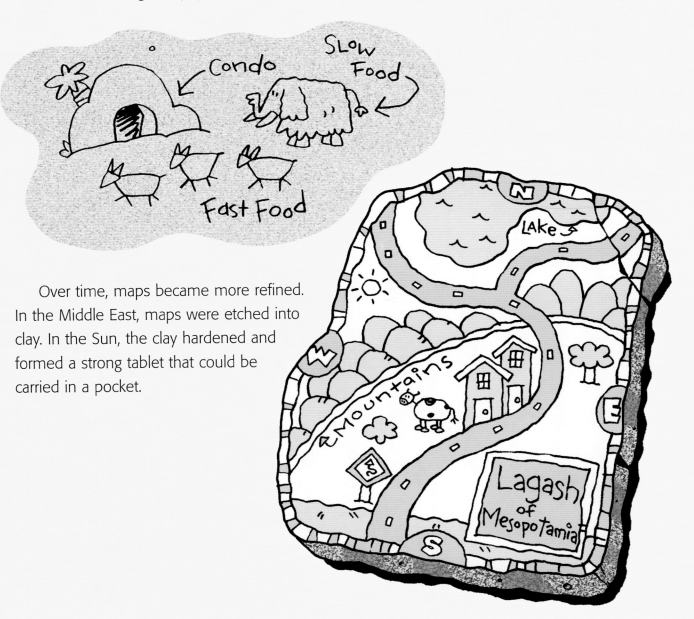

Over time, maps became more refined. In the Middle East, maps were etched into clay. In the Sun, the clay hardened and formed a strong tablet that could be carried in a pocket.

Some of the most interesting maps were created by the people who lived in the Polynesian Islands. These maps are called stick charts and they were used to navigate the ocean. Leaves and reeds were woven into a pattern that showed the ocean current and wave directions. Islands were represented by seashells.

Around 1400 to 1500, compasses hit it big in Europe. There were also major improvements in maps. No longer were maps based solely on tales or stories. Now, mathematical measurements could be used to make accurate maps.

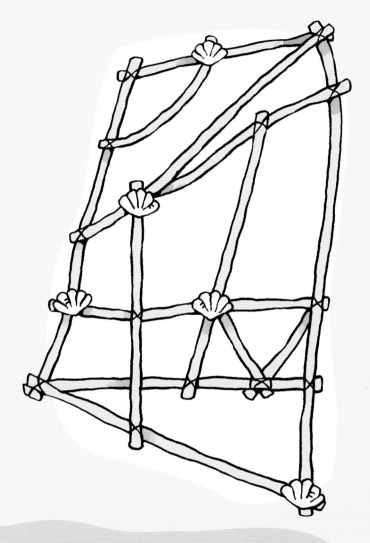

MAP FACT

An ancient Greek mathematician and astronomer named Eratosthenes figured out a way to use shadows to measure the circumference (perimeter) of the Earth with incredible accuracy. His estimate of Earth's circumference was off by less than 100 miles. Not bad for a calculation made over 2000 years ago!

Let's Get Physical (and Political)

Although there are many different types of maps, two kinds are most often plastered to the classroom walls. One type of map is called a *political map*. The political map is based upon boundaries that are established by governments.

The political map doesn't show how the land really looks. In fact, most of the time the countries or states are colored in different pastel shades to help tell the countries apart. The political map shows boundaries and locations of cities, towns, roads, and major land features such as rivers, mountains, and high peaks.

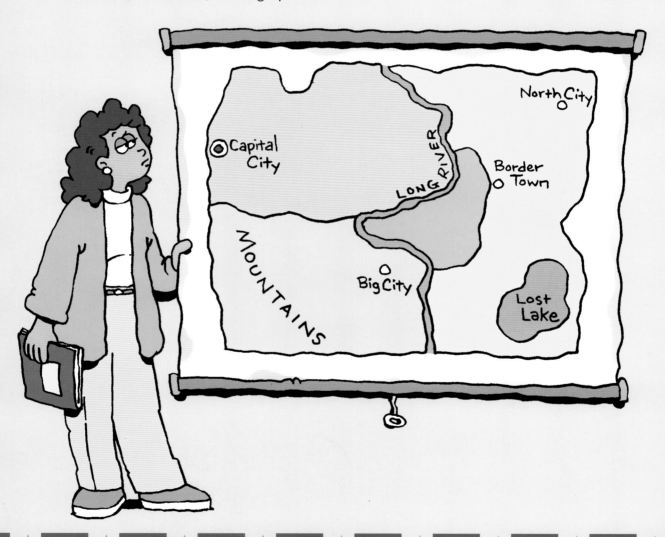

The other type of map is called a *terrain* or *physical map*. This map tries to show how the land features might appear if they were viewed from an orbiting spacecraft. Sometimes borders and cities are drawn in.

Get your granola ready: Most physical maps use "earthy" colors or patterns to represent different elevations or natural things such as trees and deserts.

MAP FACT

Towards the end of the 1800s, map trading cards became a hit. Similar to today's baseball cards, they were collectable items. At the time, most map cards were given away or included as "gifts" within such items as one-pound coffee bags.

The Ups and Downs of Topos

May we present the most awesome mountain this side of the universe: Mount Kid.

On a political map, Mount Kid might look like:

To better understand a

Either way, there isn't a wealth of information about the mountain's shape, slope, or terrain.

In order to see the "ups" and "downs" of the land, you need a topographic map—or "topo" for short. Unlike other maps, the topo has *contour lines*. They trace out the specific elevations of a terrain.

Here's a topographic map of Mount Kid. Each of the contour lines identifies an eleva-

On a physical map, Mount Kid might look like:

tion. These contours are measured in meters and separated by an interval of 500 feet.

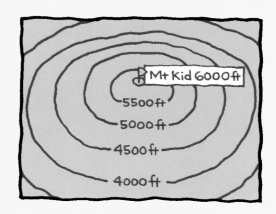

topographic map, let's build the following with a lump of clay, different-colored yarns, a pencil, and a ruler.

1. Shape the clay into a fist-sized mountain.
2. Hold the pencil point level at a height of ½ inch (or approximately 1 cm).
3. Poke a series of ½-inch (1-cm)-high marks around the mountain.
4. Place a "ring" of yarn around the marks.
5. Hold the pencil point at a height of 1 inch (2 cm).
6. Poke a series of 1-inch (2-cm) marks around the mountain and connect them with a different color of yarn.
7. Continue raising the pencil and placing marks until the top of the mountain is reached.

To get a topographic view, look straight down on the mountain top. The yarn rings represent contour lines. Contour lines that are positioned close together show a quick, or steep change in the land. Contour lines that are spaced more apart represent a slow, gradual slope.

Slicing Up the Earth

Have you ever tried to cover a small ball with a sheet of graph paper so that all of the grid squares kept their same size, shape, and position? If so, it wasn't easy. In fact, it is downright impossible.

There are hundreds of ways that mapmakers have tried to show curved features on a flat map. All of these different methods are called *projections*.

One type of projection is based upon making slices called *gores*. Suppose you sliced the globe as if it were an orange. Then you "peeled" the sections and laid the skins side to side. You would have a map that looked something like this:

Want to see how twelve gores fit together into a spherical earth? Just follow these directions:
Trace or photocopy this set of gores. Cut them out along their outlines. Wrap and tape the gore strip around a table tennis ball. Gather and tape the pole ends together. Presto, a globe…kind of. It isn't perfectly round, but you get the point.

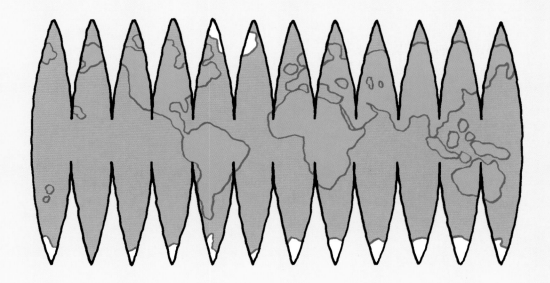

MAP FACT

The word "map" comes from the Latin word for "cloth," because this was the material that many of the ancient maps were drawn on.

Gorey Details

Although gores show features with little distortion, their flat layout is awkward to use. Parts of continents and huge chunks of ocean are missing. The simplest way to repair this is to "fill in" the spaces with extra land and water.

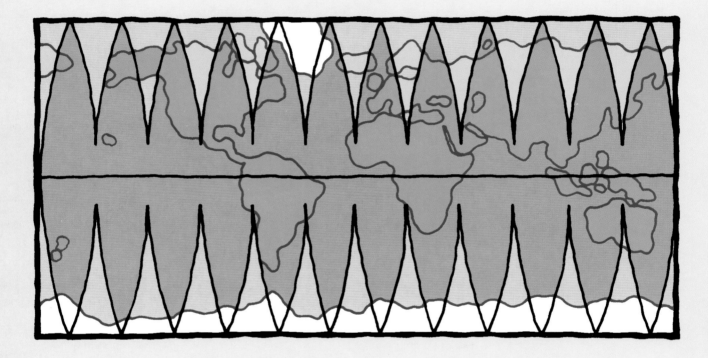

Although the "filled-in" map is easier to use, it is very distorted. The regions near the poles get plenty of added surface. This makes polar regions of this map projection seem much larger than they really are.

STRETCHING THE TRUTH

The style of map below is called a *Mercator Projection*. For more than 400 years, the Mercator Projection has been used to show the globe's flattened features.

From this map, most would agree that North America appears larger than Africa. But if you measured the actual continents, you'd find that North America occupies about 19 million square kilometers while Africa occupies 30 million square kilometers.

Now compare the sizes of Greenland and South America. According to this map, Greenland is slightly bigger than South America. But if you measured the actual land masses, you'd be surprised: South America is EIGHT TIMES larger than Greenland!

Find the equator. This line should separate the Earth into two equal halves: an upper half and a lower half. Yet the equator is drawn below the midline of the map. This distortion makes the Northern Hemisphere countries appear bigger while countries South of the equator look smaller.

Why? Because the Mercator Projection was developed by a European. It reflects a European-centered view of the world.

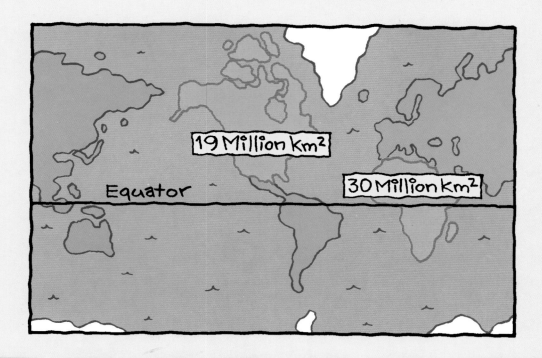

19 Million km²

30 Million km²

Equator

Map Mania

The first BIG road map was made by:

a) Monks who had "pushed" the limits of paper folding

b) Romans who needed to move armies

c) A used car dealer who needed to stop things from rattling around in the glove compartment.

Answer is b. Although they had no cars, the ancient Romans had plenty of roads. About 2000 years ago, someone drew a road map of the Roman Empire. It was over 20 feet long and about a foot wide. The map showed a distorted network of 70,000 miles of road.

LEAVING HOME

Imagine our country's roads a century ago. They were dusty, uneven, full of holes, and mostly unmapped. Nothing more than trodden paths, roads were routes you followed to visit friends or get to the equivalent of today's local mall—the country store.

Then came the automobile, which changed things around. Suddenly, people were leaving their home turf and traveling beyond their local neighborhood.

Realizing that the auto-generation needed to know where they were (and where they were going), road maps were created. The first commercial road maps appeared around 1905 and were made by companies with an interest in selling automobiles and car products. Tire and oil industries were first to mass produce these maps.

Pilot to Navigator

It's getting late. You've been traveling for hours along an endless route of streets, highways, and back roads. Then, without warning, the driver says from the behind the wheel, "Take the road map from the glove compartment and read it."

You do that easily but then comes the responsibility of reading the map. But that's no big deal compared to the later responsibility of folding the map back the way you found it.

Puzzle Break

This map consists of four side-by-side panels. In how many different ways can you fold it?

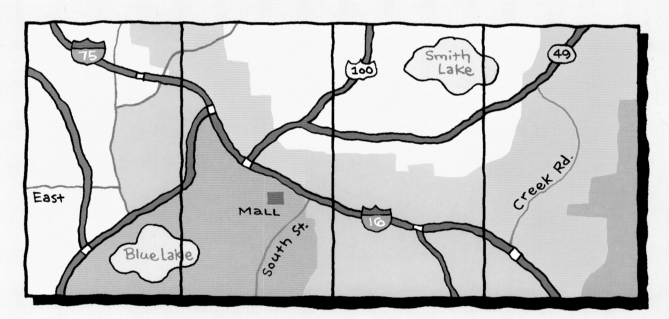

Hint: Don't try and visualize all the potential folds. Instead, grab a piece of paper of similar shape and start folding!

Answer on page 79.

Where in the Map?

B-2. BINGO!

Wasn't that the winning call in last night's bingo game? Perhaps, but it's also a shortcut to locating Nowheresville.

Many maps have a time-saver for finding towns and cities. It's called an *index*. The index lists the names of places in alphabetical order. Each place is assigned a locator combo. Most often, this combo contains two parts: a letter (B) and a number (2).

Here's part of the index for the map on the next page:

Cities

Noplace D2

Nowheresville . . . B2

Plain Lost F4

Gonesville . . . . . .

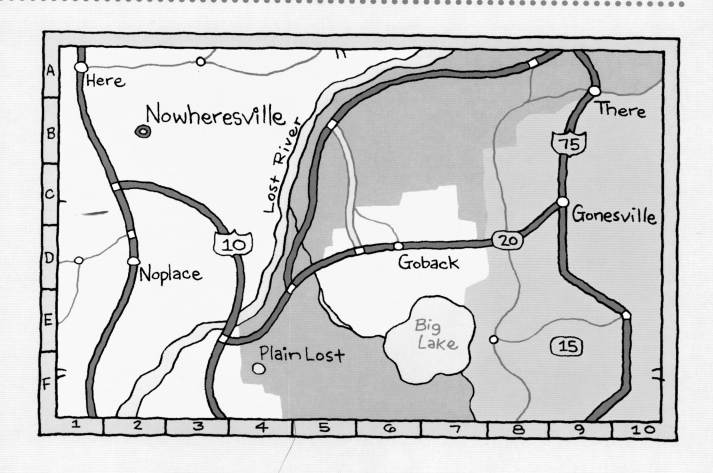

What's the Buzz with B? The Clue with 2?

The map is divided up into a box-like grid. Rows run left to right. Columns (like building supports) go up and down.

Each row is given a different letter. The uppermost row is A. The next row down is B. Next is C, and so on.

Each column is given a different number. The first column on the left is 1, next is 2, next is 3, and so on.

Nowheresville is found in the second column and second row: B-2.

Mom! Dad! How Much Longer? (I need a rest stop!)

"Does this road go to Atlanta?"

"Sorry, but this road doesn't go anywhere. It stays right here."

"But can I take this road to Atlanta?"

"Leave it put. Atlanta has too many roads as it is!"

Have you ever tried to use your thumb to measure the exact distance of a route on a road map? It's almost impossible, unless you're some sort of slimy invertebrate (in-VUR-tuh-briht). If you were a squid, you'd have no problem in curving your rubbery tentacle along the anything-but-straight roadways. So what's a vertebrate (VUR-tuh-briht) to do?

Most maps have tiny numbers that are printed next to the roads. These numbers give the distance in miles between the neighboring dots. To get a longer distance, just add up the segment miles.

QUICK QUIZ

Check out the map here. How many miles is the shortest road trip from Anyplace to Whereabouts?

Answer on page 79.

ARE WE THERE YET?

There's also another timesaving trick that is included on some maps. It's called a mileage table.

	Anyplace	Gottago	Noplace	Nowheresville	Plain Lost	Tire Flats	Wieremeye?
Anyplace		18	8	24	22	13	20
Gottago	18		21	18	25	18	26
Noplace	8	21		12	11	20	5
Nowheresville	24	18	12		10	13	12
Plain Lost	22	25	11	10		12	7
Tire Flats	13	18	20	13	12		8
Wieremeye?	20	25	5	12	7	8	

To use this chart, locate your starting point in a column. Now find your destination in one of the rows. The intersection of the row and column gives a number. This number is the driving distance in miles between the two places. For example, what's the distance in miles between Plain Lost and Nowheresville? 10 miles!

Lost in Space: Transmission Intermission

SPACE MAPS

It's strange but True: NASA has launched several road maps into space. Why? To show space aliens where Earthlings live.

These maps are tacked onto the sides of space probes. After exploring the planets of our solar system, these craft follow a path into deep space. Scientists hope that any ETs (short for extra-terrestrials) who discover these drifting probes will have read the alien version of *Map Mania* (called ^%&*&%^&^$^##*090).

With the book as a reference, the ETs should know enough about maps to decode the diagram and locate Earth.

HELLO DAVE

Unexpectedly, you awake from your state of suspended animation. You are tired, hungry, and ticked off that your spacecraft isn't back at Earth. Unfortunately, your computer has suffered a minor memory lapse. It must be programmed to direct your craft on a course to our solar system.

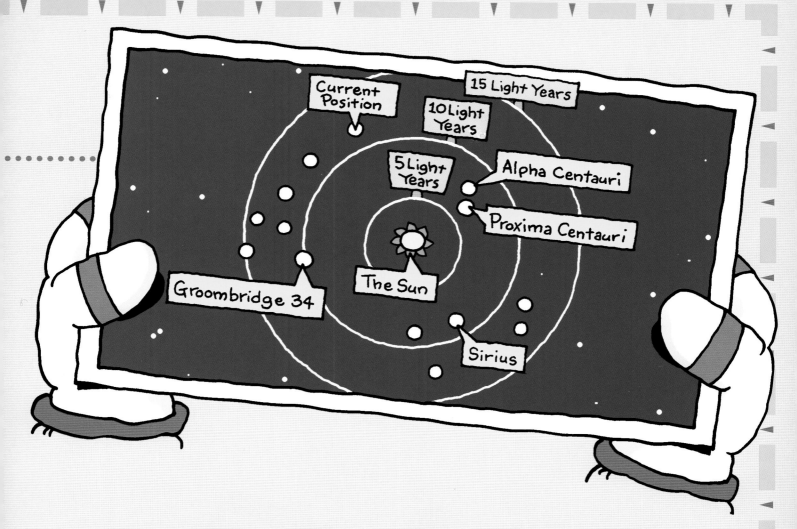

The computer displays a cool map of many hot stars. Your destination is the star labeled "Sun." Before you can input your course heading, the computer (affectionately nicknamed HAL) wants to engage you in small talk. HAL's needs are simple, its motives selfish, and its power absolute. Answer HAL's questions and you'll be set on your course back to Earth.

HAL: 1. What is the distance from our current position to the Sun?

HAL: 2. Let's say I goofed (oh my) and overshot our Sun by a scant 8 light years. Where would we be then?

HAL: 3. Let's say I was upset when we arrived at our Sun. I didn't stop, but instead took a right turn and kept on going for about 10 light years. Where would we make our new home?

Answers on page 79.

Help from Above

GPS is a:

a) A new 3-D video game platform.
b) A top secret military location finder.
c) An instrument (or system) that can pinpoint your position anywhere on the planet.

The answer is "C." GPS stands for Global Positioning System. It's a high-tech way to find any location on Earth. There are two main parts to GPS:

1. GPS satellite. There are over twenty GPS satellites in orbit above the Earth. Each satellite follows its own track. As it circles the planet, it transmits a radio signal to the ground. But don't try to tune in on this signal with an AM/FM radio. The GPS signal isn't music or talk. It's more like brrrrrrrrrrrr… brrrrrrrrrrrrrrrr… brrrrrrrrrrrrrrrr.

2. GPS receiver. This device picks up the signal from four different GPS satellites at the same time. It analyzes these signals to uncover the exact location of the receiver.

So if you hold a GPS receiver in your hand—whether you're at the beach, hiking in the mountains, in the bathroom, at Grandma's, in gym class, hanging out on top of the Empire State Building, wherever—the GPS receiver can tell you where you are.

WHAT'S MY LINE?

The GPS gives your location in latitude and longitude measurements. Remember them? The horizontal lines are called *latitude*. These lines tell how far North or South something is. They are also called parallels (which shouldn't be too much of a stretch since these lines are parallel to each other). Some of the more important latitudes are:

1. The equator: 0 degrees latitude. It's the big one. The latitude which encircles the girth, or the widest part, of the planet.
2. 90 degrees North: Welcome to the North geographic Pole.
3. 90 degrees South: It's the South geographic Pole.

The up and down lines are called *longitude*. These lines tell how far East or West something is. Unlike lines of latitude, the longitude lines aren't parallel. All of them join up at both the North and South Poles.

Think back to school. If you learned about any longitude line, it was probably the one from which all others are measured. This reference longitude line is called the *prime meridian*. It has a measure of 0 degrees longitude and runs right through a broom closet of a fancy observatory in Greenwich, England.

MAP FACT

Over 2000 years ago, some Greek guy named Hipparchus was the first to use a system of latitude and longitude lines.

Tool Time 2

Wouldn't it be great if this book came with a GPS receiver? You bet, until we discovered that the cheapest GPS system costs around $100. That would make this book really, really, really expensive.

So we headed back to the drawing board and came up with our own affordable version of this satellite system. It's called an astrolabe, and it was invented by ancient Greeks nearly 2000 years ago.

Up until the middle ages, the astrolabe was a popular tool that navigators used on their trips. Later on, the astrolabe got replaced by a fancier instrument called the *sextant*, which has some extra parts, including a telescope and mirror system. The extra parts make the sextant easier and more reliable to use.

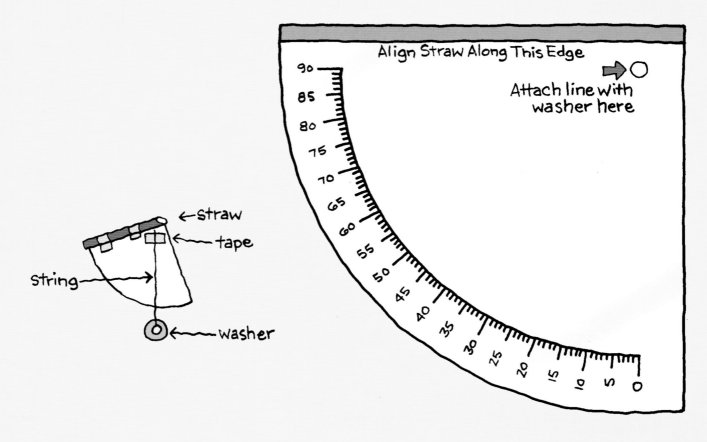

BUILDING AN ASTROLABE

To build an astrolabe, you'll need to get the following materials: straw, tape, string, washer, and scissors.

Are you kidding?—you may be thinking. You can uncover your latitude and longitude using only these cheap materials?

Kind of. Everything has a trade-off. (Isn't an old TV better than no TV? Aren't brussels sprouts better than no food?) Our astrolabe can only tell you your latitude. And since it's physically impossible to provide you with extensive sky charts within this book, your astrolabe will only work half the time: At night.

THE INSIDE STEPS

1. Photocopy or trace the astrolabe scale onto a sheet of heavy stock paper.
2. Use scissors to trim the scale along its outline.
3. Tape the straw onto the scale as shown in the drawing. Trim both edges of the straw so they don't stick out beyond the edge of the paper scale.
4. Tie a piece of string (about one foot long) to a metal washer.

5. Tape the other end of the string to the "X" of the scale.
6. Hold out the astrolabe so that the weighted string falls freely. Note where the string crosses the measurement scale.

THE OUTSIDE STEPS

1. Wait until evening, then step outside with a friend. Locate Polaris (see page 34–37).
2. Put on safety goggles. Look at Polaris through the straw opening of your astrolabe.
3. As you look at Polaris have your friend read the measurement where the string crosses the astrolabe scale. This measurement is your latitude!

WARNING!

When looking through your astrolabe, always wear eye protection and never look at the Sun or other very bright targets!

Lost!

By now, you have probably become somewhat of an expert on finding your way. You've learned all sorts of tricks and tactics that will prevent you from ever getting lost. Great job! Nicely done!

However…no matter what you do, things like keys, wallets, and homework assignments always seem to get misplaced. No matter how careful you are, you're bound to lose something!

The following are the five things reported most often lost on New York City trains and buses. Do any of these items look familiar? If so, you might want to give them a call and claim your lost property.

- Backpack
- Radio/Walkman®
- Eyeglasses
- Wallet and
- Pocketbook

Can you guess what item might be next on this list?

a) Umbrella   c) Keys

b) Shoes   d) Camera

The answer is:

a) Sorry. But umbrellas did make the top ten lost property list of the London Transport.
b) Although shoes are not next, they did walk away with one of the top ten spots.
c) A close call. Although a good number of keys are lost, many people don't report them missing. (Anonymous keys have few clues to the doors they unlock.)
d) Cameras. Smile! That's the right answer.

STRANGE BUT TRUE

The Lost and Found list for the London Transport includes a:

- Human skeleton
- Box of glass eyes
- Outboard motor
- Burial urn containing someone's ashes
  (which was never claimed).

Bermuda Triangle

Vanishing without a trace! Ghost ships! Weird vibes!

Would you steer a course through the Bermuda Triangle?

The Bermuda Triangle (aka the Devil's Triangle) is a region of sea located in the Atlantic Ocean. The "official" area is found between three corners of a huge and very wet triangle. The bottom corners of this triangle are placed at San Juan, Puerto Rico and Miami, Florida. The triangle's top corner is located at (you guessed it) Bermuda.

But is it a simple coincidence that the name of the triangle and the name of the uppermost corner are the same, or is it something more… something supernatural?

Some people believe that the Bermuda Triangle forms a rip in the fabric of space! Boats, planes, and house keys that disappear into this "passageway" emerge at the other end of the universe. Other people think that the Bermuda Triangle is a short-term parking lot for visiting UFOs who on occasion scoop up people and cruise the galaxy with them.

In the mid-1960s, the "supernatural" powers of the triangle were brought to the public's attention. Stories suggested that hundreds of disappearances could be attributed to the strange powers of this tract of ocean. There was only one big problem (actually, two) with believing this account:

1. The disappearances can also be explained by more natural means, such as storms, leaks, collisions, faulty compasses, and an annoying lack of gas stations found in open ocean.

2. Many of the disappearances took place outside of the triangle. Events that occurred in far away places, such as the waters off New England, South America, Ireland, and Europe were seen as part of the triangle's long and mysterious reach. Even disappearances in the Pacific and Indian Ocean were offered as proof of the triangle's expanding powers!

TRIANGLE'S MOST FAMOUS LOST SHIP

In 1892, sailors discovered one of the best-known ghost ships of all time, the Mary Celeste. This ocean-crossing vessel was apparently abandoned by its ten member crew (along with the lifeboat). Some say that ghosts scared the sailors from the ship. Others insist that the crew was late for a party on Alpha Centuri. But many believe that the Mary Celeste was another victim of the Bermuda Triangle. Oooooooooooo. Too bad the ship was found off the coast of Portugal—nowhere near the Bermuda Triangle. Even its trans-Atlantic course was way north of the Bermuda Triangle.

A more rational explanation suggests that the captain and crew were bad guessers. When a storm hit the ship, they may have mistakenly thought that the vessel would sink, so they prematurely abandoned ship.

Mary Celeste

The Disappearance of Flight 19

Do you like a good story? Everyone does, including the film director Steven Spielberg. He used the "reappearance" of Flight 19 to begin his popular alien contact movie, *Close Encounters of the Third Kind*.

THE TALE

It's December 5, 1945. On this perfectly still night, a group of five dive-bombers takes off from their Florida air base on a typical training mission. Each plane of Flight 19 is flown by an experienced two-man crew. The planes are equipped with state-of-the-art navigation devices and radio transmitters.

While they are flying the mission, something goes wrong. The patrol leader sends out an S.O.S. call. His bizarre message states that the Sun is in the wrong place.

An "unsinkable" rescue seaplane is sent out to find Flight 19 and rescue the pilots. This seaplane and all of its crew disappears. By evening's end, twenty-seven men and six planes have been swallowed by this mysterious stretch of ocean. Although the waters of the coastal Florida are shallow and crystal clear, no wreckage is located.

Topsy-turvy Truth

Sometimes facts get turned upside down. Yes, on this night, six planes did not return from their base. However, when you learn more about the disappearance, the story becomes less mysterious.

THE FACTS

- Except for the patrol leader, the crews were rookies. They had very little flying experience.
- The weather was not calm. There was a major storm and rough seas.
- The patrol leader did not have a compass and probably wasn't wearing a watch.
- Most likely, the leader thought that the patrol was over the Gulf of Mexico and ordered his crews to fly East, believing that they would cross the Florida mainland.

- A "fix" *was* taken of the planes. It placed them about 300 miles East of Florida.
- The leader's wrong directions sent his inexperienced crew Eastward into the stormy blackness of the Atlantic Ocean.
- Several witnesses saw the search plane explode soon after takeoff. Oddly, that wasn't bizarre. These rescue seaplanes were known for leaky gas lines that often blew up!

SO ANSWER ME THIS THEN

Question: If these planes crashed into the shallow seas off Florida, why hasn't any wreckage been found?

Answer: The patrol probably flew so far East that it placed them beyond the shallow coastal waters. Any wreckage would have sunk thousands of feet beneath the ocean's surface, making it very difficult to locate.

Lost Dutchman Mine

"No miner will find my mine."

Thanks for the encouragement, Pops.

"There is a trick in the trail to my mine."

Who buried this gold, Penn and Teller?

"To find my mine, you need to pass a cow barn."

That certainly narrows down the location.

For over 100 years, people have searched for the lost mine of Dutchman Jacob Waltz (who was actually German, but liked being called "Dutchman"). Legend has it that somewhere in the Superstition Mountains east of Phoenix, Arizona, this prospector left an incredible cache of gold. It was also rumored that on his deathbed, he gave a bunch of mysterious clues that could lead anyone to his stashed treasure!

Some say that Waltz discovered a rich vein of gold and secretly mined it for 10 years. Others believe that he bought a map to an old Mexican gold mine. Still others think that Waltz came across gold treasures that the Spaniards had stashed away centuries before.

Although Waltz was definitely a real person, many believe his mine may not have been as real. Skeptics believe that the Lost Dutchman Mine is nothing more than a fib. Just imagine cowpokes sitting around the camp fire, eating beans, and sharing late night stories. Wouldn't a romantic tale of a lost gold mine brighten the evening?

But even people who have doubts about the mine are sure that Waltz was on to something. When he died, there was about 50 pounds of gold ore hidden under his bed. Where did it come from?

GOLD FEVER, ANYONE?

Perhaps you've thought of looking for this lost treasure? Well, don't hold your breath. Because even if you found his treasure, you couldn't have it. Years ago, the U.S. government made this region of the Superstition Mountains off-limits to prospecting and mining.

When Being Lost Is Where You Want To Be

MUTINY ON THE BOUNTY

A mutiny is pretty serious business. So when you decide to take a ship away from its captain, you better be able to find a pretty good hiding spot (or have enough cash on hand to hire a great lawyer).

About 200 years ago, an officer by the name of Captain Bligh commanded the British ship *H.M.S. Bounty*. During its months at sea, the *Bounty* bopped around the South Pacific. After a while, some of the crew decided that an extended stay in a tropical paradise was far better than returning home to not-so-jolly England. Under the leadership of first mate Fletcher Christian, they mutinied.

Taking command of the ship, the mutineers placed Bligh and his loyal sailors in one of the *Bounty*'s lifeboats. They lowered away the lifeboat and off went Bligh in one direction. The *Bounty* (with its mutinous crew) went in the other direction.

MISTAKEN MAPMAKERS

The mutineers knew that the British navy wouldn't look favorably upon their action. In fact, warships, carrying a hangman's noose for each of the mutineers, would soon be searching for them.

Needless to say, the rebels needed a good spot to hide. What they uncovered, however, was the absolute best hiding place!

They found an island that was misplaced. Who misplaced it? The mapmakers. Somehow the mapmakers drew this island in the wrong place. Therefore, every chart in the British navy showed this island exactly where it wasn't. The only way to find this place was by accident!

Without too much discussion, the mutineers decided to stay in a place that no one knew how to find. To firm up the crew's decision, the *Bounty* was set afire and sunk.

LOCATING A LOST LOCATION

This home picked by the mutineers was an isolated spot called Pitcairn Island. It's about 3000 miles East of New Zealand. At the time, the only way you could find this island was by accident. Nowadays, just use a GPS system and set your sights on latitude 25 degrees, 4 minutes South and longitude 103 degrees and 6 minutes West.

Lost Continent of Atlantis

Sure, it's easy to lose things that aren't very big. Pocket toys, coins, and social studies reports seem to have an unnatural way of disappearing. It's even reasonable to forget where you parked a car. But how do you lose a continent?

THE STORY

Plato was an ancient Greek who liked to think. (Actually he would have loved to veg out on MTV, but he was several thousand years too early.) He also liked to tell stories. One of his stories was about a great empire called Atlantis. According to Plato, Atlantis unsuccessfully attacked Greece. Following its defeat, the continent was destroyed by earthquakes and floods, and eventually it sank beneath the surface of the sea.

As years went by, the legend of Atlantis became bigger and better. No need to tell a small story when you can make up a BIG ONE! Soon, Atlantis

was considered a lost world populated by an advanced race. The many Atlantis-related stories include:

- The grandparents of most Atlanteans arrived by UFO.
- Atlanteans didn't speak. They communicated by thought waves.
- Dead Atlanteans talk to modern-day people through spirit channels.
- Atlantis was destroyed in 1500 B.C. by nuclear war and death rays.

SO WHERE IN THE WORLD IS (OR WAS) ATLANTIS?

Pick one:

- Mid-Atlantic Ocean. Plato said that it was West of Europe. That would place it somewhere out in the Atlantic Ocean. Maybe it was part of the Azores Islands. These islands are about 900 miles due West of Portugal. Or maybe it was even further out there (certainly the stories are).
- Mediterranean. Just South of Greece is the volcanic island of Thera. Around 1500 B.C., the island blew up. This explosion might have caused the downfall of a huge and powerful civilization that Plato had called Atlantis.
- Plato's imagination. Even before modern-day politicians, storytelling was a wonderful art.

THE DISAPPOINTING NEWS DEPARTMENT

So far, there is no archeological proof that Atlantis definitely existed.

My Grandchild is Atlantean

Lost Treasure of Oak Island

Everyone loves tales of lost treasure. Perhaps the most mysterious and bizarre treasure story rises from the beach of Oak Island.

THE MONEY PIT

Imagine strolling along the shore of an isolated beach. You look down at the ground beneath your feet and find yourself standing in the middle of a perfect circle of sand. Strange. There shouldn't be any sand here. But there is, and it appears as if this sand was used to fill a round hole that was dug into the dirt.

You look above the hole and see a tree with a sawed-off limb. Mysterious.

For years, you have heard tales of buried pirate treasures. Possibly, this is one of them. You return home and get a couple of friends to help you.

When you return to the hole, you start digging. Two feet down you uncover a layer of flat stones. Ten feet down, there's a platform of logs. You keep digging and find two more log platforms at 20 and 30 feet. Tired of digging, you make a secret pact with your friends and plan to return as soon as possible.

Neither you nor your friends are great at keeping appointments. Eventually, you return—8 years later. This time, you're a grownup who happens to own a mining company and have access to grownup things, like money.

Your mining company takes up where you and your two buddies left off years ago.

Down you go. Every 10 feet you find another layer of logs. Enough with the logs already! You also dig through a layer of charcoal, putty, and coconut fibers. At 90 feet, you find a neat stone that has mysterious writing. You continue digging, thinking the treasure can't be much deeper!

Then suddenly, without warning, water begins flowing into the pit! By the next day, the water has flooded the pit. Pumping out the water doesn't work, because more water replaces the pumped water. And digging a new hole that's dug right next door doesn't work, because water also seeps into that. You then give up.

This story is true. It happened 200 years ago on the beaches of Oak Island. Oak Island is located off the coast of Nova Scotia, Canada.

BOOBY TRAP

It turns out that the money pit was booby trapped! When the trap was sprung, sea water rushed in through a secret, 500-foot underground waterway connecting the pit to a nearby cove. Many believe that the booby trap was created to prevent hunters from discovering the pit's riches. But what are those riches? To this day, no one seems to know. But considering all the work that went into building the pit and booby trap, the treasure was probably worth plenty!

LOST AND FOUND DEPARTMENT

Who lost this treasure? No one really knows. However, there are at least four neat theories. We've listed those theories below and added one of our own. Can you tell which one of the following we made up?

1. Captain William ("Billy" to you) Kidd. This infamous pirate is rumored to have buried his treasure on Oak Island.

2. First National Pirate Bank. The association of seagoing pirates got together and created their own version of Fort Knox.

3. High Order of Loch Ness. These Scottish monks buried the body of the last Loch Ness monster in a remote grave site that would most likely remain undisturbed.

4. The French. During their New World exploits, they needed a neighborhood bank branch that was unlikely to be lost to the English.

5. The Lost Treasure of Peru. With the help of European friends, the Incas may have removed and safeguarded their culture's treasure from the conquistadors.

Answer on page 79.